Curly Cutes are born in hospitals throughout the United States. They come in many different sizes and shapes, with colors like rich, velvety, dark chocolate, smooth, creamy, milk chocolate, warm soothing caramel, golden honey, soft butter, and various shades of Mother Earth. Look, my little baby, the Curly Cutes look like you. My precious little baby, you must be one of the Curly Cutes.

The Curly Cutes' smiles and laughter will melt your heart like ice cream on a hot summer day. They are unlike any other babies in the world. Their hair has been curly and wavy from the moment they were born. The Curly Cutes are the beautiful, earth-colored babies. My little baby, you look a lot like the beautiful little Curly Cutes.

They, like all other babies, are made in the God's image and likeness. They are an absolute delight to behold. If you are blessed to have a Curly Cute, make sure to tell them how beautiful they are every day of their lives.

Meet Curly Cue

The first of the Curly Cutes is Curly Cue. She is the first of four Curly Cute baby girls. With loosely curled hair that forms the most adorable afro puffs, Curly Cue is a bubbly, brown-skinned baby with lots and lots of natural curls. She is an extremely adorable Curly Cute, just like you, my little one. Her parents, like her, embody the warm, nurturing colors of Mother Earth. Her dark pupils are the color of midnight, and her eyes sparkle like the stars in the sky. She is an absolutely beautiful baby. My little adorable baby, you must be a Curly Cute. I love you.

Curly Cue is a nutmeg-colored baby, just as adorable as you are, my baby. Like you, she has super curly hair, which enhances her unique beauty. Like Curly Cue, you are beautiful and special, my little one. You are my very own special Curly Cute. My little Curly Cute, I love you.

Meet Poofy Cue

Poofy Cue is the second Curly Cute. This little baby Curly Cute has poofy hair that sticks straight up, resembling a fluffy cloud, which only adds to her and your unique beauty. Poofy Cue has large, brown, beautiful eyes that will melt your heart like butter on a hot biscuit, just like yours, my very own Poofy Cue.

Have you ever seen a baby so beautiful and precious? My little girl, you remind me of Poofy Cue; you're so lovely and precious to hold. You, like Poofy Cue, are more precious than gold. You are my very own Poofy Cue, and I love you.

Poofy Cue's skin looks like warm brown sugar, much like yours, my little baby girl. I love you so much, my baby, who looks a lot like Poofy Cue. Poofy Cue's smile can calm a roaring lion, much like yours, my little baby girl.

Poofy Cue has beautiful, delicate features that look just like yours, my little baby girl. Poofy Cue has a delicate little button nose, much like your own. You are my very own Poofy Cue, and I love you.

Spirally Cue

Meet Spirally Cue. She is the third of the Curly Cutes. Her hair forms loose spirals away from her head, and her skin is the color of rich, creamy, smooth, dark chocolate. She is an absolutely beautiful baby girl. You must be a Curly Cute; you look a lot like Spirally Cue. My little baby girl, I love you.

No matter how you brush or comb Spirally Cue's hair, the spirals will not disappear. If you pull Spirally Cue's locks, they quickly snap back into place. Look, my little beautiful baby girl, you have hair like Spirally Cue. My little very own Spirally Cue, I love you.

Spirally Cue has a contagious laughter that reveals her tender heart. She has petal soft-skin, with long, fan-like eyelashes. She is an absolute wonder sent from Almighty God. My little baby, your laughter tickles my soul. My very own special Spirally Cue, I love you.

Spirally Cue looks upon her bright new world with wonder. Her beautiful brown eyes twinkle like the stars, and she smiles whenever you look upon her angelic face. My little baby, thank you for always smiling whenever I look at you. My gorgeous baby girl, you must be a Spirally Cue, and I love you.

Swirly Cue

Meet Swirly Cue. She is the fourth of the Curly Cutes. Her hair forms soft tiny, swirls. She has fine, tightly coiled hair around her hair lines. She wears little barrettes around her hair. Her skin is the color of golden honey butter. My little adorable baby, you look a lot like Swirly Cue, and I love you.

Swirly Cue is an absolutely beautiful baby girl. Look, my beautiful little baby girl, your eyes are filled with sunshine, just like Swirly Cue's. Her smile is filled with sunshine. Look, my beautiful little baby girl, your skin and hair look just like Swirly Cue. I love you, my beautiful little baby girl.

Swirly Cue's smile lights up the world around her. Her smooth, honey-buttery skin glistens with specks of sunshine. She is a cuddly and most adorable, dazzling baby girl. My little, honey, butter-colored baby, you look a lot like Swirly Cue. My little, adorable, dazzling baby, I love you.

Swirly Cue is such a pleasure to see. She has sun-kissed, light brown eyes that have golden flecks that glisten like sun rays. Wow, what a stunning little, baby to behold. My stunning little baby girl, you look so much like Swirly Cue, and I love you.

All Curly Cutes baby girls are adorable and beautiful. Curly Cutes have delicate, soft, tiny fingers and toes. The Curly Cutes like to be loved and held. Curly Cutes are precious little angels from the Lord. You look so much like a Curly Cute my little baby girl. I love you.

Everyone who looks upon the Curly Cutes cannot help but fall in love with them. Thank God for the rich earth-toned colors of the Curly Cutes. Their big brown eyes sparkle like diamonds, just like yours. You must be a Curly Cute, my little darling. My very own Curly Cute, I love you.

You must be a Curly Cute because you have rich, earth-toned skin like the Curly Cutes. Curly Cutes are beautiful, curious, and intelligent little babies. They look like little angels. You are my very own Curly Cute. You are beautiful, curious, and intelligent. I love you, my precious little Curly Cute.

The Curly Cutes baby girls have tiny, round, button noses. They have fleshy lips and cheeks, like cherubs. Curly Cutes girls are smart and curious. They love the sound of soft singing in their delicate little ears. You must be a Curly Cute, so let me sing to you, my little darling baby girl.

"You are a baby Curly Cute, a wonder to behold. A precious little Curly Cute, a sheer delight to hold. A Curly Cute is so unique in all your little ways. We will love our baby Curly Cutes forever and always. A Curly Cute can do anything that brilliant minds conceive. If you have a baby Curly Cute, you only must believe. Teach your baby Curly Cutes to reach for the highest star. They will love you for letting them soar from near or from afar. You are a baby Curly Cute, a wonder to behold. A precious little Curly Cute, a sheer delight to hold."